Wordplay

A collection of poems for children

Published by BBC Educational Publishing,
a division of BBC Enterprises Limited,
Woodlands, 80 Wood Lane, London W12 0TT

First published 1992
© BBC Enterprises Limited 1992
Illustrations © 1990 Shirley Barker (pages 74, 75, 80, 92 and 93);
Linda Birch (pages 14, 15, 56, 57, 58, 59, 60 and 61); Rob Chapman
(pages 46, 47, 48 and 50); Michael Charlton (pages 26, 27 and 29);
Gunvor Edwards (pages 10, 12, 13 and 23); Robert 'Cleverclogs'
Green (pages 18, 19, 24, 25 and 36); Stephanie Harris (pages 63, 66
and 68); Tony Kenyon (pages 30, 31 and 33); Kevin Kimber (76, 77,
78, 79, 88 and 89); Tony Morris (pages 51, 52, 53, 70, 72, 73, 81 and 91);
Trevor Parkin (pages 80 and 90); Gwen Tourret (pages 8 and 16);
Shirley Tourret (pages 17, 38, 85, 86, 87, 94 and 95)

Cover illustration © 1992 Pippa Sterne
ISBN 0 563 34981 6
Set in Nimrod by MS Filmsetting Ltd, Frome, Somerset
Printed and bound in Great Britain by Hollen Street Press

CONTENTS

About this book

FRIENDS
Children's poems

Melanie	Poppy Toland	9
Duvet	Gus Jaspert	9
Teddy	Gus Jaspert	9
Eric my friendly cat	Tom Foot	10
All friends should be like this	Caroline Rose	10
Classifying	Judith Nicholls	11
Partners	Judith Nicholls	12
Sister √	Judith Nicholls	13
Brian's picnic	Judith Nicholls	14

FAMILIES

She read as she cradled	Lemn Sissay	17
Mickey Hackett's rocket	Leo Aylen	18
Messy Melanie's Muddy Monday	Leo Aylen	20
Flop	Leo Aylen	22
You've wounded the sky	Leo Aylen	23
Dottidreem	Leo Aylen	24
High heels	John Agard	26
Ask Mummy, ask Daddy	John Agard	27

Say cheese!   John Agard 27
The older the violin
  the sweeter the tune   John Agard 28
Drummer can't dance   John Agard 29
Our sounds   Sue Cowling 30
Video Nasties   Sue Cowling 31
Well, you shouldn't have...   Sue Cowling 32
Sickening   Sue Cowling 32
Chickenpox   Sue Cowling 34
Tricky situation   Sue Cowling 36
Granny Granny
  please comb my hair   Grace Nichols 37
Wha me mudder do   Grace Nichols 38
My cousin Melda   Grace Nichols 39
Winter and summer   Kathy Henderson 40

JOURNEYS

Magic carpet   Shel Silverstein 43
The edge of the world   Shel Silverstein 43
The long-haired boy   Shel Silverstein 44
Where the sidewalk ends   Shel Silverstein 47
The Big Rock Candy Mountains   Folksong 48
The ark   Elizabeth Jennings 49
Noah and the rabbit   Hugh Chesterman 50
The owl and the astronaut   Gareth Owen 52

Mandy likes the mud   Gareth Owen   *54*
Skipping song   Gareth Owen   *56*
Shed in space   Gareth Owen   *58*

LETTERS
Dear Maureen   Michael Rosen   *61*
I can't say that   Brian Morse   *62*
Christmas thankyou's   Mick Gowar   *64*
Ben   Colin West   *66*
Letter from YOUR SPeCIAL-
    BiG-pUPPy-Dog   James Berry   *67*
Letter from Your KitTen-
    cAT-AlMost-BiG-Cat   James Berry   *68*

ANIMALS
If only   Richard Edwards   *70*
On the move   Richard Edwards   *71*
The snake   Richard Edwards   *72*
The Sliver-slurk   Richard Edwards   *74*
A wild one   Richard Edwards   *76*
Turn, turn, turn   Adrian Mitchell   *78*
Good taste   Adrian Mitchell   *78*
The galactic pachyderm   Adrian Mitchell   *79*
Roger the Dog   Ted Hughes   *80*
Moon-whales   Ted Hughes   *81*

NIGHT

The bad dream	Jackie Kay	83
The adventures of Carla Johnson	Jackie Kay	84
Night is...	Matt Simpson	86
Still awake	Matt Simpson	88
Dropping off	Matt Simpson	89
Round and round	Matt Simpson	90
In the middle of the night	Kathy Henderson	92
A Scouser asks a question	Matt Simpson	94

Acknowledgements

ABOUT THIS BOOK

How did you learn your first words?
Who taught you?
Can you remember?
After a while, perhaps you learned to say hundreds of words.
Words that tell stories and carry messages and invent
jokes...
Words that tell your friends and your family about the ideas
in your head...
This is what poets do.
Like you, they have many things to say. So they write down
their ideas in their poems. You can read some of these poems
in this book.
When you turn the pages, you will find out what poets have to
say about friends and families ... journeys and letters ...
animals and night-time.
You can also hear the poems read out loud if you listen to the
Wordplay programmes on BBC Radio 5. After you have
listened to the programmes

- look for your favourite poems in this book and read them
  out loud to your friends
- with a group of friends, each choose a poem and make up
  your own poetry programme
- learn a poem, carry it around in your head and say it to
  your family and friends

Have fun!

Alan Lambert
BBC Producer, *Word Play*

FRIENDS

These poems are written by children.
This is what they say about their friends . . .

MELANIE

She is my best friend.
Her laugh echoes round the room
Making my mum cross.

Poppy Toland

DUVET

In times of trouble
My duvet's always a friend—
Gives me a cuddle.

Gus Jaspert

TEDDY

A true special friend
Who'd never answer me back
But just understands.

Gus Jaspert

ERIC MY FRIENDLY CAT

He wakes me up by
Rubbing his head on my feet
And biting my toes.

Tom Foot

ALL FRIENDS SHOULD
BE LIKE THIS

An anxious-listener
A friendly-cover
An animal-lover
A brainy-writer
A sweet-liker
A mystery-adventurer
A low-whisperer
An always-forgiver
A good-truster
A comforting-soother
A pleasant-talker
A polite-eater
An understanding-partner
An interesting-storyteller.

Caroline Rose

CLASSIFYING

Philip and Annie wear glasses
and so do Jim and Sue,
but Jim and Sue have freckles,
and Tracey and Sammy too.
Philip and Jim are in boys' group
and Philip is tall like Sam
whilst Jim is small like Tracey and Sue
and Clare and Bill and Fran.
Sue is in Guides and recorders,
but Clare is in Guides and football
whilst Helen fits in most things—
except she's a girl and quite tall.
Jenny is curly and blonde and short
whilst Sally is curly but dark;
Jenny likes netball, writing and maths
but Sally likes no kind of work.
Philip and Sam are both jolly,
Fran's best for a quiet chat;
now I
    have freckles, like joking, am tall,
    curly, dark, in Guides, football and
    play penny whistles and the piano . . .

how do *I* fit into all that?

Judith Nicholls

PARTNERS

Find a partner
says sir, and sit
with him or her.
A whisper here,
a shuffle there,
a rush of feet.
One pair,
another pair,
till twenty-four
sit safely on the floor
and all are gone
but one
who stands,
like stone,
and waits;
tall,
still,

alone.

Judith Nicholls

SISTER

Tell me a story!
Lend me that book!
Please, let me come in your den?
I won't mess it up,
so please say I can.
When? When? When?

Lend me that engine,
that truck—and your glue.
I'll give half of my old bubblegum.
You know what Dad said
about learning to share.
Give it now—
or I'm telling Mum!

Oh, please lend your bike—
I'll be careful this time.
I'll keep out of the mud
and the snow.
I could borrow your hat—
the one you've just got . . .
                          said my sister.
And I said   NO!

Judith Nicholls

BRIAN'S PICNIC

We've...
cheese rolls, chicken rolls,
beef rolls, ham;
choose now, quickly, Brian—
bacon, beans or spam?

I WANT A DOUGHNUT!

We've...
egg and cress and sausages,
good old lettuce leaf;
come on, Brian, take some now—
there's turkey, tuna, beef...

I WANT A DOUGHNUT!

We've...
treacle tart and apple tart,
biscuits, blackberries, cake—
Take which one you feel like,
Brian, come along now, take!

I WANT A DOUGHNUT!

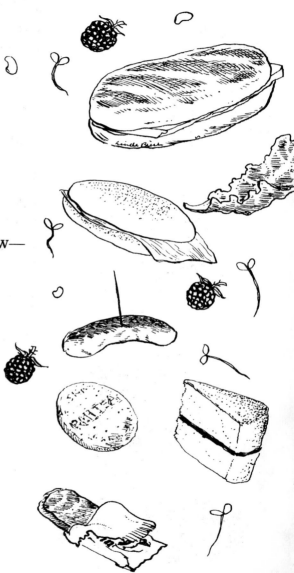

There's . . .
jelly next or trifle,
everything must go!
Quickly, Brian, pass your plate—
is it yes or no?

I WANT A DOUGHNUT!

LAST CHANCE!

We've . . .
sponge cake, fruit cake,
eat it **any** way!
Peanut butter, best rump steak . . .
What is that you say?

I WANT A DOUGHNUT!

Judith Nicholls

FAMILIES

SHE READ AS SHE CRADLED

You part of me

Every day your history
Every tomorrow your destiny
Every growth your mystery
Every mother wants a baby like you

Every laugh your personality
Every look your clarity
Every word your stability
Every mother wants a baby like you

Every hiccup a comedy
Every fall a catastrophe
Every worry my worry
Every step you're beside me
Every sight you're pure beauty
Every mother wants a baby like you

Every tear wiped carefully
Every word spoke lovingly
Every meal fed silently
Every cloth washed caringly
Every song sung sweetly
Every day I whisper quietly
Every mother wants a baby like you

Lemn Sissay

MICKEY HACKETT'S ROCKET

Mickey Hackett
Built a rocket
From a bracket
And a sprocket.
'Look, Dicky! Book your ticket.'
Dicky tried to nick it.
'I'll knock it,
Kick it,
Crack it.'
They were making such a racket,
Dad took it,
Tried to pack it
In the pocket
Of his jacket.

But Mick—'e's quick an' wicked—
Said, 'Dick, let's see you dock it.
Sneak it out and hook it
To the cooker.
Stick it
Crooked
In the socket
And tack it.'
Wow! What a shock! It
Knocked Dad back. It
Crackled,
Smoked, and blackened
A mackerel,
Some cheese crackers,
Dad's mac, a tennis racquet,
And a packet of Mum's stockings.
Mum raised a raucous ruckus,
Smacked 'em, made 'em chuck it
All mucky in the bucket.
Dad whacked 'em,
Thwacked 'em,
Kicked 'em
Up to their room and locked it.

Leo Aylen

MESSY MELANIE'S MUDDY MONDAY

This is what happened to Melanie on the day Uncle Tom took her to the park, when she should have been having her rest.

Let me slide down the slide.
Let me slide down the slide.
I like the swings,
And those circular things
Where you stand on the step and go round and round
Making sure your foot doesn't scrape on the ground,
And I like to climb on the climbing frames,
And I like all the other games,
But—coming to the park, it won't be the same,
If I don't slide down the slide.

Let me slide down the slide.
Let me slide down the slide.
I'll slide on my bottom, I'll slide on my chest.
I hadn't forgotten I'd be having my rest
If you hadn't brought me to the park instead
Of making me lie on my boring bed.
So I'm very happy I'm in the park
And not tucked up in drawn-curtain dark,
'N I love the way you push me so high

On the swings, my feet fly up in the sky,
'N you *don't* mind my shoelace isn't tied,
So please,
Let me slide down the slide.

Ooh! Ooooh!!

OOOOOOOOOOOOOOOOOOOOOOOOOOOH!!!!!!!!!!
I slid on my bottom. I slid on my chest.
There's mud on my jeans. I've torn my vest.
I scratched my hand. My bottom's sore.
But, please, let me slide just . . . a thousand times more.
Sliding the slide's the best of all.
I don't mind I lost my ball.

And though
I know
We've got to go,
I've . . . just once more . . . climbed
The steps, and I'm . . .
Sliding down one last time.

When we got home, Mum screamed and shouted at Uncle
   Tom
'You fool, get out!
What have you done to the child? She's hurt.
There's mud on her jeans, there's mud on her shirt.
She's cut her hand. She's lost a shoe.
What you did was a horrible thing to do.
When I found she wasn't asleep in bed,
I nearly went off my head.

You're a thoughtless bully. Go away.
And never come back.'
I slipped behind where he'd hung his mack,
And took my uncle's hand, and said:
'Today was the wonderfullest wonderfullest day,
And I wish you'd always take me to play.'

But I never saw Uncle Tom again
For a million years—till I was ten.

Leo Aylen

FLOP

In a bucket of black water
Was reflected a star.
'Stars are enormous, lad,
And ever so far.'

While the boy was watching,
Their donkey called Flop
Stuck his head in the bucket of water,
And drank every drop.

'Dad, what marvellous creatures
Little donkeys are.
Flop's belly is extra-terrestrial.
It can swallow a star.'

Leo Aylen

YOU'VE WOUNDED THE SKY

'You've wounded the sky'
The child cried
As he woke from his sleep.
'You told us lies,
And you wounded the sky'
He said again, and began to weep.
When his mother asked him 'Why
Did you say what you said?'
He could only reply
'You've wounded the sky,
And soon it will be dead.
And soon we'll all be dead'.

Leo Aylen

DOTTIDREEM

Last night I dreamt of welly boots
In a sea of chocolate spread.
Then I dreamt of a ginger cat who hoots
Her horn at kids in bed.

Then I dreamt of a collie dog with a bone
Which flew to the moon and back.
Then the bone turned into a telephone,
And told me I must pack,

'Cause we were off for our holidays
In a place called Custard Sol,
Where they serve you custard in fifty-seven ways.
Then a three-legged, talking, doll

Told me 'If you are very good,
You can have an elephant ride.
Run down the hill to the middle of the wood,
And shout 'Your chips are fried.'

But the elephant shrank to beetle size,
And whispered down its trunk:
'Please pour some ketchup on my mince pies,
And please don't say I'm drunk.'

Then all at once the elephant—
And the dog with the bone, and the cat—
Sang *Three Blind Mice* to a rubber plant
Wearing a three-cornered hat.
But the rubber plant, growing very angry,
Put them all in its big tea-cup,
And pounced on me, saying 'Aren't you hungry?'
Luckily, I woke up.

Leo Aylen

HIGH HEELS

I wonder
how it feels
to wear high heels
like my big sister?

Coz I'm smaller
I have to wait
longer
for high heels
to make me taller.

I wonder
how it feels
to wear high heels
and have corns
on your toes
and a blister?

I suppose
I'd better
ask my big sister.

John Agard

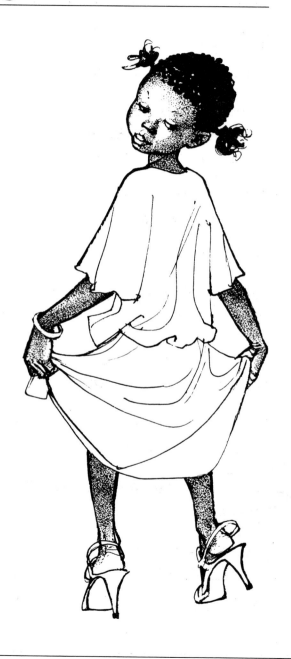

ASK MUMMY ASK DADDY

When I ask Daddy
Daddy says ask Mummy

When I ask Mummy
Mummy says ask Daddy.
I don't know where to go.

Better ask my teddy
he never says no.

John Agard

SAY CHEESE!

Take a picture of me
and let my Mummy see.

Take a picture of me
Please, please, please!

But I don't wanna say cheese
and smile.

I wanna say ice-cream
and SCREAM!

John Agard

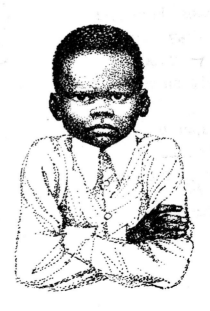

THE OLDER THE VIOLIN
THE SWEETER THE TUNE

Me Granny old
Me Granny wise
stories shine like a moon
from inside she eyes.

Me Granny can dance
Me Granny can sing
but she can't play the violin.

Yet she always saying,
'Dih older dih violin
de sweeter de tune.'

Me Granny must be wiser
than the man inside the moon.

John Agard

DRUMMER CAN'T DANCE

I'm always doing
too many things at once
Like brushing my teeth
and trying to sing
Like sucking sugarcane
and trying to whistle
Like doing homework
and playing scrabble
Granny would ask,
'You ever see somebody dance
and play drum-kit?'
Yes, Granny,
I bet you I do it.
Just give me a drum-kit!

John Agard

OUR SOUNDS

The people in our family
each have a favourite sound.
Dad likes the noise of money chinking
5p, 10p, pound.
I like the bell of my new blue bike
and the rattle of the doorkeys.
The dog likes a sort of biscuity sound
and a voice that calls out 'Walkies'.
Kate likes to hear the rain drum
and the buzzing of the 'phone,
and Mum—? She loves the silence
when she's in all on her own.

Sue Cowling

VIDEO NASTIES

One of my brothers is Batman
it's brilliant the way he goes ZOOM!
the other thinks he
is Karate Kid 3—
when he's Back from the Future
or the Temple of Doom!

When 'there's something strange
in the neighbourhood'
who ya gonna call—?
MY SISTERS!
they'll zap you all
if you don't agree
that I'm really (you guessed it!)
Crocodile Dundee.

We're so video-mad in our family
that even our pets get ideas!
The fish thinks he's Jaws—
does the dog think he's Paws?
and the rabbit—? Well, he must be ... EARS!

Sue Cowling

WELL, YOU SHOULDN'T HAVE ...

Mum—I've just had an explosion.
   Well, you shouldn't have shaken your drink!

Mum—I've just flooded the bathroom.
   Well, you shouldn't have blocked up the sink!

Mum—I've just spilt Grandad's maggots.
   Well, you shouldn't have been in the shed!

Mum—I've just tidied my bedroom.
   Well, you shouldn't have ... WHAT'S that you said?

Sue Cowling

SICKENING

He's always kicking things
my brother
stones
the back gate
me when Mum can't see

He's always flicking things
my brother
crumbs
ink pellets
cold peas from his plate

He's always picking things
my brother
scabs
his toenails
worst of all, his nose

and if it's none of these
he's
tricking me
mimicking me
nicking what belongs to me
never sticking up for me

He's sickening
my brother.

Sue Cowling

CHICKENPOX

Spots spots
one two three
are coming out
all over me!
four five six
bet this will fix them
seven eight nine
we'll calomine them
spots spots
lots and lots
from head to toe
they still won't go

I've just found
half a dozen more
they're getting bigger
than before
spots   spots
thick and fast
don't know
how long they last
so please
don't
stand too near
or you
might
catch ... oh dear!

Sue Cowling

TRICKY SITUATION

Sister Jean likes
sticking on stamps
she gives them lots of licks!

Brother Mike's
not half so keen—
he'd sooner be stamping on sticks!

Sue Cowling

GRANNY GRANNY PLEASE COMB MY HAIR

Granny Granny please comb
my hair
you always take your time
you always take such care

You put me on a cushion
between your knees
you rub a little coconut oil
parting gentle as a breeze

Mummy Mummy
she's always in a hurry-hurry
rush
she pulls my hair
sometimes she tugs

But Granny
you have all the time
in the world
and when you've finished
you always turn my head and say
'Now who's a nice girl'.

Grace Nichols

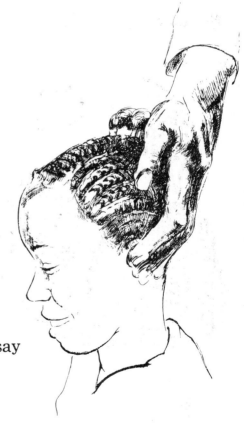

WHA ME MUDDER DO

Mek me tell you wha me Mudder do
wha me mudder do
wha me mudder do

Me mudder pound plantain mek fufu
Me mudder catch crab mek calaloo stew

Mek me tell you wha me mudder do
wha me mudder do
wha me mudder do

Me mudder beat hammer
Me mudder turn screw
she paint chair red
then she paint it blue

Mek me tell you wha me mudder do
wha me mudder do
wha me mudder do

Me mudder chase bad-cow
with one Shoo
she paddle down river
in she own canoe
Ain't have nothing
dat me mudder can't do
Ain't have nothing
dat me mudder can't do

Mek me tell you

Grace Nichols

MY COUSIN MELDA

My cousin Melda
She don't make fun
She ain't afraid of anyone
even mosquitoes
when they bite her
She does bite them back
and say—'Now tell me, how you like that.'

Grace Nichols

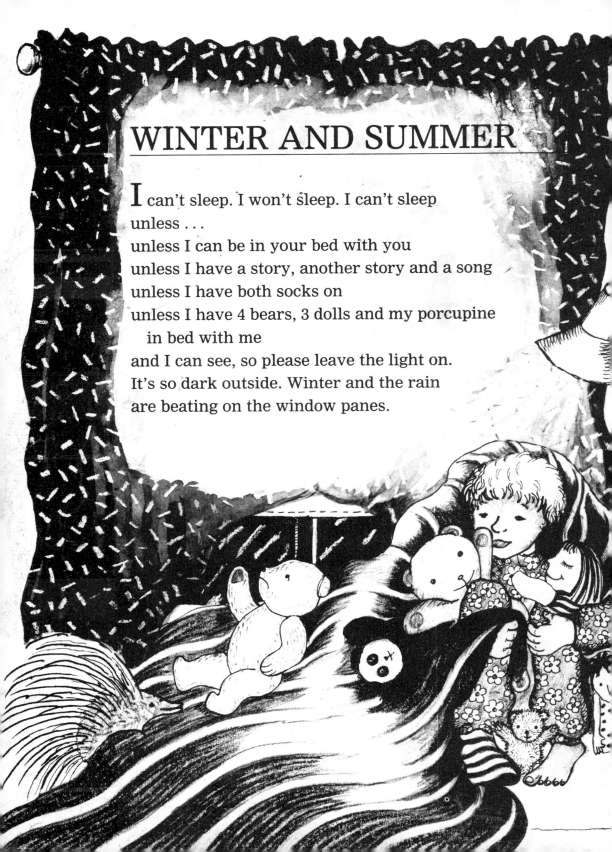

WINTER AND SUMMER

I can't sleep. I won't sleep. I can't sleep
unless . . .
unless I can be in your bed with you
unless I have a story, another story and a song
unless I have both socks on
unless I have 4 bears, 3 dolls and my porcupine
   in bed with me
and I can see, so please leave the light on.
It's so dark outside. Winter and the rain
are beating on the window panes.

I won't sleep. I can't sleep. I won't sleep
because . . .
because it's summer
because it's light outside (this blind doesn't fool me)
because I can hear cars and buses
   and a blackbird singing from a rooftop TV aerial
because I'm lonely
because I'm hot
because mum's not home yet.

You're still up anyway. So why
should I
go to sleep?

Kathy Henderson

JOURNEYS

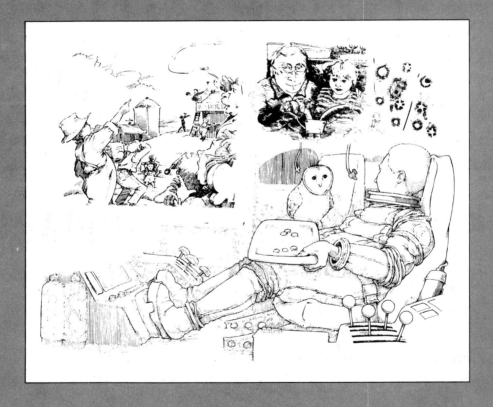

MAGIC CARPET

You have a magic carpet
That will whizz you through the air,
To Spain or Maine or Africa
If you just tell it where.
So will you let it take you
Where you've never been before,
Or will you buy some drapes* to match
And use it
On your
Floor?

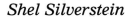

Shel Silverstein

*drapes is the American name for curtains

THE EDGE OF THE WORLD

Columbus said the world is round?
Don't you believe a word of that.
For I've been down to the edge of the world,
Sat on the edge where the wild wind whirled,
Peeked over the ledge where the blue smoke curls,
And I can tell you, boys and girls,
The world is FLAT!

Shel Silverstein

THE LONG-HAIRED BOY

There was a boy in our town with long hair—
I mean really long hair—
And everybody pointed at him
And laughed at him
And made fun of him.
And when he walked down the street
The people would roar
And stick their tongues out
And make funny faces
And run in and slam their door
And shout at him from the window
Until he couldn't stand it anymore.
So he sat down and cried
Till his whole body shook,
And pretty soon his hair shook too,
And it flapped
And flapped—
And he lifted—
And flew—

Straight up in the air like a helicopter.
Jenny Ricks saw him and dropped her
Knitting and screamed, 'It's a flying kid!'
Lukey Hastings ran and hid
Under Old Man Merrill's car,
Miss Terance fainted, Henry Quist

Tried to shoot him down, but missed—
'I thought he was a crow,' he said.
And 'round he sailed all through the day,
Smiling in the strangest way,
With the wind in his hair
And the sun in his eyes.
We saw him swoop and bank and rise.
He brushed the tree-tops
And skimmed the grass
On Yerbey's lawn and almost crashed
Right into Hansen's silo*—but
Zoomed up in time and almost hit
The courtyard. Old Man Cooley bit
Right through his napkin when he saw
A kid fly through the diner door—
And out of the window, tipping the ladder—
Where Smokey was painting, he almost had a
Heart attack—he clung to a rafter.
The kid flew on—
Us runnin' after,
Cheering and sweating
And screaming, 'Hooray!'
Mayor Lowry shouted, 'Hey—
Come down here, kid. We'd like to say
How proud of you we are today.
Who ever thought our little
Town would have a hero in it?
So I'd like to proclaim this day—hey, kid!

*a silo is a place for storing grain

Will you please come down for just a minute?'
But the flying kid did not come down.
He treaded air above the town,
Sort of cryin' and looking down
At all of us here on the ground.

Then up he flew, up into the clouds,
Flapping and flying so far and high,
Out past the hills and into the sky
Until a tiny speck against the sun
Was all we could see of him . . . then he was gone.

Shel Silverstein

WHERE THE SIDEWALK*
ENDS

There is a place where the sidewalk ends
And before the street begins,
And there the grass grows soft and white,
And there the sun burns crimson bright,
And there the moon-bird rests from his flight
To cool in the peppermint wind.

Let us leave this place where the smoke blows black
And the dark street winds and bends.
Past the pits where the asphalt** flowers grow
We shall walk with a walk that is measured and slow,
And watch where the chalk-white arrows go
To the place where the sidewalk ends.

Yes we'll walk with a walk that is measured and slow,
And we'll go where the chalk-white arrows go,
For the children, they mark, and the children, they know
The place where the sidewalk ends.

Shel Silverstein

a sidewalk is the American name for a pavement
**asphalt is a bit like tar: it's used for covering pavements*

THE BIG ROCK CANDY MOUNTAINS

One evening as the sun went down
And the jungle fire was burning,
Down the track came a hobo* hiking.
And he said, 'Boys I'm not turning,
I'm headed for a land that's far away,
Beside the crystal fountains,
So come with me, we'll go and see
The Big Rock Candy Mountains.'

In the Big Rock Candy Mountains,
There's land that's fair and bright,
Where the handouts grow on bushes,
And you sleep out every night.
Where the boxcars** are all empty,
And the sun shines every day
On the birds and the bees,
And the cigarette trees,
And the lemonade springs
Where the bluebird sings
In the Big Rock Candy Mountains.

American folksong

a hobo is a person who travels from place to place
**a boxcar is the American name for a railway wagon*

THE ARK

Nobody knows just how they went.
They certainly went in two by two,
But who preceded the kangaroo
And who dared follow the elephant?

'I've had enough,' said Mrs Noah.
'The food just won't go round,' she said.
A delicate deer raised up his head
As if to say, 'I want no more.'

In they marched and some were sick.
All very well for those who could be
On the rough or the calm or the middle sea.
But I must say that ark felt very thick

Of food and breath. How wonderful
When the dove appeared and rested upon
The hand of Noah. All fear was gone,
The sea withdrew, the air was cool.

Elizabeth Jennings

NOAH AND THE RABBIT

'No land,' said Noah,
'There is not any land.
Oh, Rabbit, Rabbit, can't you
understand?'

But Rabbit shook his head:
'Say it again,' he said;
'And slowly, please.
No good brown earth for burrows,
And no trees;
No wastes where vetch and rabbit-
parsley grows,
No brakes, no bushes
and no turnip rows,
No holt, no upland, meadowland
or weald,
No tangled hedgerow and no
playtime field?'

'No land at all—just water,' Noah
replied,
And Rabbit sighed.
'For always, Noah?' he whispered,
'Will there be
Nothing henceforth for ever but the sea?
Or will there come a day
When the green earth will call
me back to play?'
Noah bowed his head.
'Some day . . . some day,' he said.

Hugh Chesterman

THE OWL AND THE ASTRONAUT

The owl and the astronaut
Sailed through space
In their intergalactic ship
They kept hunger at bay
With three pills a day
And drank through a protein drip.
The owl dreamed of mince
And slices of quince
And remarked how life had gone flat;
'It may be all right
To fly faster than light
But I preferred the boat and the cat.'

Gareth Owen

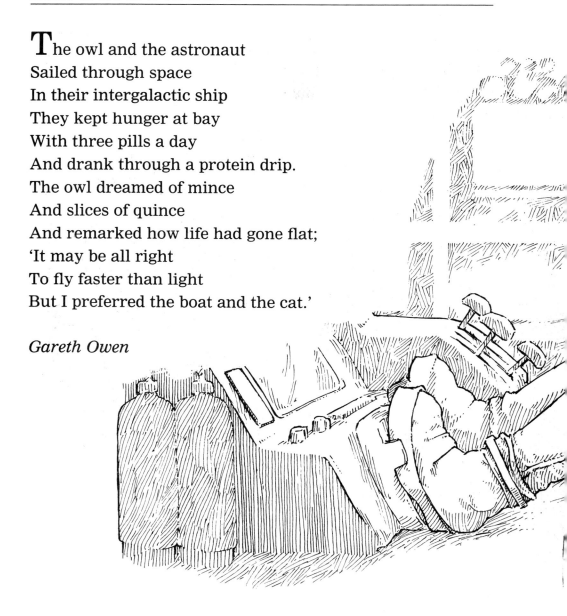

MANDY LIKES THE MUD

Polly likes to play with toys
Melissa makes a lot of noise
Ann has a bike
Trevor a trike
But Mandy likes the mud.
She jumps in it
She slumps in it
She scoops it in her hands
She rides on it
She slides on it
She digs to foreign lands.

Kevan likes to kick a ball
Peter never plays at all
Tina cooks tarts
Donna plays darts
But Mandy loves the mud.
She galumphs in it
She splarges
She glugs and slurps and slops
She grins in it
She swims in it
She does smacking belly flops.

Tricia talks to her teddy bear
Belinda combs her doll's long hair
Tracy plays tennis
Mark is a menace
But Mandy adores the mud.

She dives in it

She thrives in it

She paints it on the wall.

Gareth Owen

SKIPPING SONG

Ann and Belinda
Turning the rope
Helen jumps in
But she hasn't got a hope
Helen Freckles
What will you do
Skip on the table
In the Irish stew
Freckles on her face
Freckles on her nose
Freckles on her bum
Freckles on her toes
Helen Freckles
Tell me true
How many freckles
Have you got on you
One two three four five six seven
And out goes you.

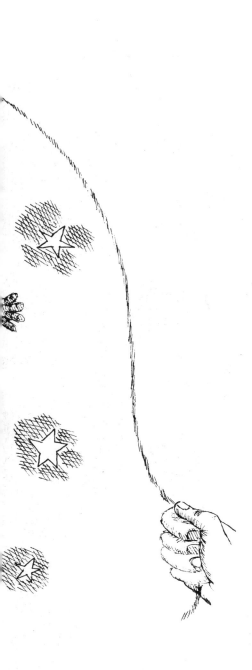

Stella Starwars
Skip in soon
Into your spaceship
And off to the moon
Skip on the pavement
One and two
Skip like a rabbit
Or a kangaroo
Skip so high
You never come down
Over the steeples
Over the town
Skip over rooftops
Skip over trees
Skip over rivers
Skip over seas
Skip over London
Skip over Rome
Skip all night
And never come home
Skip over moonbeams
Skip over Mars
Skip through the Milky Way
And try to count the stars
One two three four five six seven
Out goes you.

Gareth Owen

SHED IN SPACE

My Grandad Lewis
On my mother's side
Had two ambitions.
One was to take first prize
For shallots at the village show
And the second
Was to be a space commander.
Every Tuesday
After I'd got their messages,
He'd lead me with a wink
To his garden shed
And there, amongst the linseed
And the sacks of peat and horse manure
He'd light his pipe
And settle in his deck chair.
His old eyes on the blue and distant
That no one else could see,
He'd ask,
'Are we A O.K. for lift off?'
Gripping the handles of the lawn mower
I'd reply:
'A O.K.'

And then
Facing the workbench,
In front of shelves of paint and creosote
And racks of glistening chisels
He'd talk to Mission Control.
'Five-Four-Three-Two-One-Zero—
We have lift off.

This is Grandad Lewis talking,
Do you read me?
Britain's first space shed
is rising majestically into orbit
From its launch pad
In the allotments
In Lakey Lane.'

And so we'd fly,
Through timeless afternoons
Till tea time came,
Amongst the planets
And mysterious suns,
While the world
Receded like a dream:
Grandad never won
That prize for shallots,
But as the captain
Of an intergalactic shed
There was no one to touch him.

Gareth Owen

LETTERS

DEAR MAUREEN

Dear Maureen,
  I am a lamp-post.
  Every Saturday evening at five o'clock
  three boys
  wearing blue and white scarves
  blue and white hats
  waving their arms in the air
  and shouting,
  come my way.
  Sometimes they kick me.
  Sometimes they kiss me.
  What should I do
  to get them to make up their minds?
  Yours bewilderedly,
  Annie Onlight.

Michael Rosen

I CAN'T SAY THAT

Dear Auntie Beryl,
    Thanks for the Christmas present.
    It was lovely—
    except twenty-four-piece puzzles are much too easy
    for my age.
    Mum's put it away for the baby.
I can't say that.

Dear Pen Pal,
    Thanks for your letter.
    You've got very nice handwriting.
    Your holiday in the Bahamas sounded smashing.
    We went to Weston this year
    and it rained every single minute
    except the afternoon we were going home.
I can't say that

Dear Santa,
    There's a whole string of presents
    I'd really like to have
    But why were the only ones I got last year
    the little ones?
I can't say that.

Dear Teacher,
    I think it's a very good idea
    to practise writing letters,
    but I already know
    where to put the address and the date
    and the postcode and the 'Yours sincerely',
    and the 'With love from'—

    it's the bit in-between I find difficult.
I can't say that.

Brian Morse

CHRISTMAS THANKYOU'S

Dear Auntie
    Oh, what a nice jumper
    I've always adored powder blue
    and fancy you thinking of
    orange and pink
    for the stripes
    how clever of you

Dear Uncle
    The soap is
    terrific
    So
    useful
    and such a kind thought and
    how did you guess that
    I'd just used the last of
    the soap that last Christmas brought?

Dear Gran
    Many thanks for the hankies
    Now I really can't wait for the flu
    and the daisies embroidered
    in red round the 'M'
    for Michael
    how
    thoughtful of you

Dear Cousin
  What socks!
  and the same sort you wear
  so you must be
  the last word in style
  and I'm certain you're right that the
  luminous green
  will make me stand out a mile

Dear Sister
  I quite understand your concern
  it's a risk sending jam in the post
  But I think I've pulled out
  all the big bits
  of glass
  so it won't taste too sharp
  spread on toast

Dear Grandad
  Don't fret
  I'm delighted
  So don't think your gift will
  offend
  I'm not at all hurt
  that you gave up this year
  and just sent me
  a fiver
  to spend.

Mick Gowar

BEN

Ben's done something really bad,
He's forged a letter from his dad.
He's scrawled:

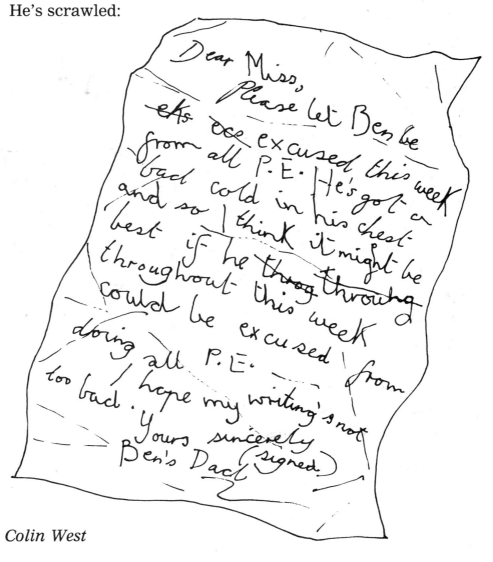

Colin West

Letter from YOUR SPeCIAL-BiG-pUPPy-Dog

You know I'm so big
I'll soon become a person.
You know I want to know more
of all that you know. Yet
you leave the house, so, so often.
And not one quarrel between us.
Why don't you come home ten times
a day? Come tell me the way
your boss is bad? See me sit,
listening, sad? And you know,
and I know, it's best
when you first come in.
You call my name. And O
I go starry-eyed on you,
can't stop wagging, jumping,
holding, licking your face,
saying, 'D'you know—d'you know—
you're quite, quite a dish!'
Come home—come call my name—
every time thirty minutes pass.

James Berry

Letter from Your
kitTen-cAT-AlMost-BiG-Cat

You tell me to clear up
the strings of wool off
the floor, just to see how
I slink out the door. But O
you're my mum. Fifty times
big to climb on. You stroke
my back from head to tail.
You tickle my furry throat,
letting my claws needle your
side,
and my teeth nibble your hand
till I go quiet. I purr.
I purr like a poor boy
snoring, after gift of a dinner.
I leap into your lap only
to start everything over.

James Berry

ANIMALS

IF ONLY

If I could be a grunting pig,
I would, and with my snout I'd dig
Deep down into the muddy ground
And deeper still until I found
A big potato, fat and sweet,
And then I'd eat and eat and eat
And when I'd eaten every bit
I'd fall asleep and dream of it:
That big potato, fat and round,
Deep down beneath the muddy ground.
Oh, with my snout I'd dig and dig . . .
If only I could be a pig.

Richard Edwards

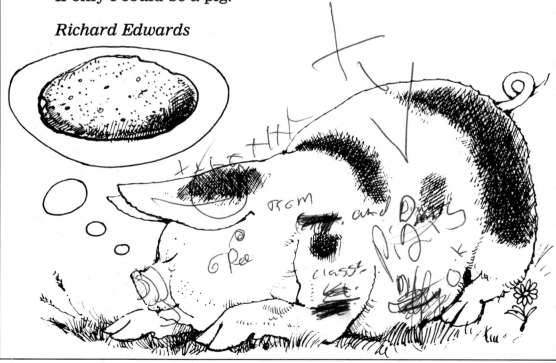

ON THE MOVE

Can't stop; hurry, scurrying
Underneath the day,
Got to hide myself before
The sun gives me away,
Got to find some shelter
Where the hungry hawk can't prey,
Can't stop; hurry, scurrying
Underneath the day.

Can't stop; hurry, scurrying
Underneath the night,
Got to hide myself before
The moon's too big and bright,
Got to find some shelter
Where the beastly fox can't bite,
Can't stop; hurry, scurrying
Underneath the night.

Can't stop; hurry, scurrying
Always moving hole,
How long can I last before
This rushing takes its toll?
Wonder if in heaven
There'll be time to lounge and stroll;
One thing's sure: whoever made this world
Was not a vole.

Richard Edwards

THE SNAKE

I hate the snake
I hate the snake
I hate the way it trails and writhes
And slithers on its belly in the dirty dirt and creeps
I hate the snake
I hate its beady eye that never sleeps.

   I love the snake
   I love the snake
   I love the way it pours and glides
   And essses through the desert and loops necklaces
   on trees
   I love the snake
   Its zigs and zags, its ins and outs, its ease.

I hate the snake
I hate the snake
I hate its flickering liquorice tongue
Its hide and sneak, its hissiness, its picnic-wrecking spite
I hate its yawn
Its needle fangs, their glitter and their bite.

I love the snake
I love the snake
I love its coiled elastic names
Just listen to them: hamadryad, bandy-bandy, ladder,
Sidewinder, asp
And moccasin and fer de lance and adder

And cascabel
And copperhead
Green mamba, coachwhip, indigo,
So keep your fluffy kittens and your puppy-dogs,
I'll take
The boomslang and
The anaconda. Oh, I love the snake!

Richard Edwards

THE SLIVER-SLURK

Down beneath the frogspawn,
Down beneath the reeds,
Down beneath the river's shimmer,
Down beneath the weeds,
Down in dirty darkness,
Down in muddy murk,
Down amongst the sludgy shadows
Lives the Sliver-slurk;

Lives the Sliver-slurk
And the Sliver-slurk's a thing
And a clammy kind of cling,
With a row of warts on top
And a row of warts beneath
And a horrid way of bubbling through
Its green and stumpy teeth;

With its green and stumpy teeth,
Oh, the Sliver-slurk's a beast
That you'd never find invited
To a party or a feast—
It would terrify the guests,
Make them shake and shout and scream,
Crying: 'Save us from this loathesomeness,
This monster from a dream!'

It's a monster from a dream,
Haunting waters grey and grim,
So be careful when you paddle
Or go happily to swim:
It is down there, it is waiting,
It's a nasty piece of work
And you might just put your foot upon
The slimy Sliver-slurk.

Richard Edwards

A WILD ONE

I heard him rustling about in the leaves
In a ditch at the edge of the wood.
He was square,
He was covered with hair,
He squeaked
And he sometimes leaked,
He could stand on one leg
And he sat up to beg
When I tickled his feathery tail,
His tummy was warm, his nose was cold,
I had no idea of his age,
His eyes were like buttons of burning gold
And I took him and built him a cage.

I papered it, polished it, planed it and put
A saucer of cream on the floor.
But he pined,
He sniffled and whined,
He sat
And his tail went all flat,
He hid in the straw

And he scratched at the door
Whenever I entered the room.
He cowered in a corner, crawled and crept,
He never once wanted to play,
He watered cream with his tears when he wept
And his bright eyes began to turn grey.

I put him back under the leaves of the ditch
And he whisked away into the wood.
He was square,
He was covered with hair,
He squeaked
And he sometimes leaked,
He could stand on one leg
And he sat up to beg
When I tickled his feathery tail,
His tummy was warm, his nose was cold,
I had no idea of his age,
His eyes were like buttons of burning gold
And he didn't belong in a cage.

Richard Edwards

TURN, TURN, TURN

There is a time for considering elephants
There is no time for not considering elephants

Adrian Mitchell

GOOD TASTE

The vilest furniture in this land
is an elephant's foot umbrella stand

Adrian Mitchell

THE GALACTIC PACHYDERM

The elephant stands
   among the stars
He jumps off
   Neptune
bounces off
   Mars
to adventure on
   Venus
while his children
   play
in the diamond jungles
   of the
Milky Way

Adrian Mitchell

ROGER THE DOG

Asleep he wheezes at his ease.
He only wakes to scratch his fleas.

He hogs the fire, he bakes his head.
As if it were a loaf of bread.

He's just a sack of snoring dog.
You can lug him like a log.

You can roll him with your foot.
He'll stay snoring where he's put.

I take him out for exercise.
He rolls in cowclap up to his eyes.

He will not race, he will not romp.
He saves his strength for gobble and chomp.

He'll work as hard as you could wish
Emptying his dinner dish.

Then flops down flat, and digs down deep,
Like a miner, into sleep.

Ted Hughes

MOON-WHALES

They plough through the moon-stuff
Just under the surface
Lifting the moon's skin
Like a muscle
But so slowly it seems like a lasting mountain
Breathing so rarely it seems like a volcano
Leaving a hole blasted in the moon's skin

Sometimes they plunge deep
Under the moon's plains
Making their magnetic way
Through the moon's interior metals
Sending the astronaut's instruments scatty

Their music is immense
Each note hundreds of years long
Each complete tune a moon-age
So they sing to each other unending songs
As unmoving they move their immovable masses

Their eyes closed ecstatic

Ted Hughes

NIGHT

THE BAD DREAM

Mammy's face is cherries.
She is stirring the big pot of mutton soup
singing I gave my love a cherry
it had no stone
I am up to her apron
I jump onto her feet and grab her legs
like a huge pair of trousers.
She walks round the kitchen lifting me up.

Suddenly I fall off her feet.
And mammy falls to the floor.
She won't stop the song
I gave my love a chicken it had no bone
I run next door for help.
When me and Uncle Alec come back
Mammy's skin is toffee stuck to the floor.
And her bones are all scattered like toys.

Jackie Kay

THE ADVENTURES OF CARLA JOHNSON

She always says night then love I'll leave
your door open. I always sneak out of bed and close it.
Every step I take has to be quiet as held in breath.
I cannot afford a pin dropping, the shock of a sneeze.
So when I close the door it takes me half an hour
to make it from my bed and back again.
So slow to avoid the cat's miaow of the door
then it's tip toe over the threadbare carpet.

When it's dark in my room my friend
Carla Johnson comes. She has wings,
fabulous things, the colour of kiwi fruit and tangerines.
She wakes me up; come on Carla (we have the same name),
taps me on the shoulder.
We fly out the window, quiet as burglars.

We only fly to places with good names
that begin with the same letter of the alphabet.
On a single night we covered Alaska, Alabama
Albania; tonight is Louisiana, Lithuania and Largs
because I went there when I was four:
strictly speaking, it is not a nice name.
Far from being tired in the morning
I feel quite rejuvenated—no jet lag whatsoever.

Jackie Kay

NIGHT IS ...

Headlights switched on in cars
in the thickening dark,
children shouted in from play
emptying the park;

lights flicked on in bedrooms,
suddenly street lamps humming,
curtains getting swished across,
The Sandman coming;

putting fresh pyjamas on,
tucking in the sheet,
stories from a story book,
hot-water-bottle feet!

head upon the pillow,
trying to settle down—
what's that moving on the door?
just a dressing gown!

rubbing itchy eyelids,
hugging Teddy Bear,
Want A Drink Of Water!
Mummy Someone's There!

turning over on your side,
pretending not to peep,
gone before you know it
deep-down into sleep.

Matt Simpson

STILL AWAKE

Dogs booming like guns
in echoing yards;
cats rattling bins
and squalling over scraps;
the gate, unlatched,
creaking its hinges;
a faulty street lamp blinking
orange, orange; high heels
on pavements; and a drunk
crooning a loud love song;
a smell of fish and chips.

Matt Simpson

DROPPING OFF

Shut your eyes and sleep they say—
Not so easy to obey
As Give Us a Kiss, Comb your Hair,
Eat Your Greens, Don't You Dare.

Shut your eyes and sleep they've said,
So here I am tucked up in bed
Imagining this, pondering that,
Wishing I was like our cat

Who can close her eyes at will,
Sleep anywhere—the window sill,
Up trees, behind the mower in the shed,
Or where she's now—upon my bed!

I can hear her purring there
Near my toes . . . I can hear her
Going zzzzzzz . . . going . . .
I can . . .

Matt Simpson

ROUND AND ROUND

Night follows Day,
Day follows Night,
The old world spins
From Dark to Light.

From Light to Dark
The old world goes,
When the sun's set
The moon shows.

Black replaces Blue
When Night slides in,
Blue replaces Black
When Day rides in.

When half the world's awake
The other half's sleeping,
And while they are
Dawn comes creeping.

One person's Dawn
Is Dusk to another—
Darkness creeping
In to smother.

Night follows Day,
Day follows Night,
The old world spins
From Left to Right.

From Left to Right
The old world goes,
When the sun doesn't shine
The moon glows.

Matt Simpson

IN THE MIDDLE OF THE NIGHT

This is part of a long poem about the night.

A long time after bedtime
when it's very, very late,
when even dogs dream
and there's sleep breathing through the house.

when the doors are locked
and the curtains drawn
and the shops are dark
and the last train's gone
and there's no more traffic in the street
because everyone's asleep ...

then ...

the window cleaner comes
to the high-street shop fronts
and shines at the glass in the street-lit dark.

and a dust-cart rumbles past
on its way to the dump
loaded with the last
of the old day's rubbish.

on the twentieth floor
of the office-block
there's a lighted window
and high up there
another night cleaner is
vacuuming the floor,
working nights on her own
while her children sleep at home ...

Across the town at the hospital
where the nurses watch in the dim-lit wards,
someone very old shuts their eyes
and dies:
breathes their very last breath
on their very last night ...

Yet not far away on another floor
after months of waiting, a new baby's born
and the mother and the father
hold the baby and smile
and the baby looks up
and the world's just begun ...

but still everybody sleeps ...

Kathy Henderson

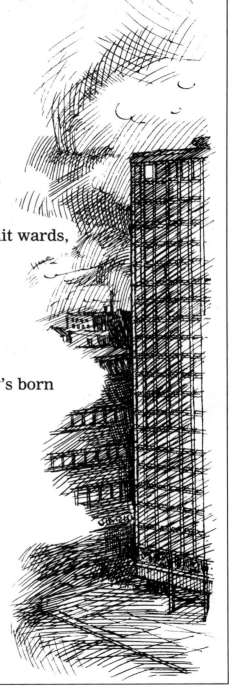

*you can read the rest of the poem in the
book called* In the middle of the night
(Walker Books, 1991)

A SCOUSER* ASKS A QUESTION

Who makes the rules up, eh?
Coz to be quite frank wid yiz
I think it's
  proper
    bloomin'
      DAFT

that every single solitary night
round about the same owld time
I gerrundrest,
  lie down,
    shut me eyes,

and become
  utterly,
    stupidly,
      boringly
        UNCONSCIOUS!

Whoever made tharrup
was either daft 'imself
or 'alf-asleep at the time.

What d'y' think, eh?

Come on, wake up, pig!

Matt Simpson

*Scouser is the nickname for someone who comes from Liverpool

Acknowledgements

Acknowledgment is due to the following, whose permission is required for multiple reproduction:

LEO AYLEN for his poems 'Dottidreem', 'Flop', 'Messy Melanie's Muddy Monday', 'Mickey Hackett's rocket' and 'You've wounded the sky'; THE BODLEY HEAD for the following poems by John Agard: 'High heels', 'Ask Mummy, ask Daddy' and 'Say cheese!' (from *I din' do nuttin'*, published by The Bodley Head) and for 'The older the violin, the sweeter the tune' and 'Drummer can't dance' (from *Say it again Granny*, published by The Bodley Head); BOGLE L'OUVERTURE PUBLICATIONS for the poem 'She read as she cradled' by Lemn Sissay; MRS JENNIFER BROWN for the poem 'Noah and the rabbit' by Hugh Chesterman, published by Basil Blackwell; FELICITY BRYAN for the poems 'On the move', 'The Sliver-slurk' and 'The snake' by Richard Edwards; WILLIAM COLLINS SONS & CO. LTD for the poem 'Christmas thankyou's' by Mick Gowar; WILLIAM COLLINS SONS & CO. LTD for the poems 'Mandy likes the mud', 'The owl and the astronaut', 'Shed in space' and 'Skipping song' by Gareth Owen from *Song of the city*, published by Fontana Young Lions/William Collins Sons & Co. Ltd (1985); SUE COWLING for her poems 'Well, you shouldn't have', 'Our sounds', 'Video Nasties', 'Sickening', 'Chickenpox' and 'Tricky situation'; FABER & FABER LTD for the poems 'Moon-whales' and 'Roger the Dog' by Ted Hughes; KATHY HENDERSON for her poem 'Winter and summer'; DAVID HIGHAM ASSOCIATES for the poem 'The ark' by Elizabeth Jennings from *The ark*, published by Carcanet; JOHN JOHNSON (AUTHOR'S AGENT) LTD for the poems 'A wild one' and 'If only...' by Richard Edwards; JACKIE KAY for her poems 'The adventures of Carla Johnson' and 'The bad dream'; DIETER KLEIN ASSOCIATES for the poem 'Scribbled notes picked up by owners and rewritten because of bad grammar, bad spelling, bad writing' by James Berry from *When I dance* by James Berry, published by Hamish Hamilton Children's Books; JUDITH NICHOLLS for her poems 'Sister', 'Partners', 'Classifying' and 'Brian's picnic'; GRACE NICHOLS for her poems 'Granny Granny please comb my hair', 'Wha me mudder do' and 'My cousin Melda' from *Come into my tropical garden*, published by A & C Black; PETERS, FRASER AND DUNLOP LTD for the poems 'Dear Maureen' by Michael Rosen and 'Good taste', 'The galactic pachyderm' and 'Turn, turn, turn' by Adrian Mitchell; ROGERS, COLERIDGE & WHITE LTD for the poem 'I can't say that' by Brian Morse; MATT SIMPSON for his poems 'A Scouser asks a question', 'Dropping off', 'Night is...', 'Round and round' and 'Still awake'; WALKER BOOKS for the poem 'In the middle of the night', text © 1991 Jennifer Eachus, illustrations © 1991 Kathy Henderson; COLIN WEST for his poem 'Ben'.

The Publishers have made every attempt to trace the copyright holders, but in cases where they may have failed will be pleased to make the necessary arrangements at the first opportunity.